LOSS TO RECOVERY

LOSS TO RECOVERY

Poems

Eden Oyelakin

ISBN: 9798333002457

ISBN 13: 9781234567897

DEDICATION

I would like to thank my God for blessing me with the ability to reach people through poetry. I thank my mother and father for their support and encouragement. Thank you to my brother for sharing his passion for poetry with me.

TABLE OF CONTENTS

<u>The Depths</u>

On the tightrope, I fell

I fell to the ground

I reached the bottom of the cliff

I stay in the depths of the ocean

I feel no emotion

On the ground, nothing is crawling

I don't make a sound

I'm no longer walking

<u>I Feel Lost</u>

I'm scared

I've lost hope, and I don't know how to cope

Deep inside me, I find no light

Deep inside I find no one for me to hide with

I'm living life guideless

On my throat, I feel a choke

In my heart, I feel a throb

Everything I cling to fades away

Everyone I loved never stayed

Walking continuously without an aim

<u>But</u>

I feel cheesy, greasy, unsafe, and without feeling

But numb I stay

I want to hide, cry, and crumble inside

But nothing I say

In my drink, my tears sink and salty it tastes

But I still drink it anyway

In my sleep, my dreams are filled with them

But when I wake up they are still far away

<u>Heavy Weather</u>

As like Summer, she burned up the skies

As like Autumn, she fell like the leaves

As like Spring, she sprong up to scream

As like Winter, it felt like the coldest cruelest snowy storm

Her feelings reformed

It ached like the whistling wind

It scarred more permanent than imprints in rocks

And till this day to no one she talks

My Very Fun Video Game

My life's a video game

I would say it's very fun to play

Except for the fact that the monsters always seem to win

Except for the fact that the hero quits

Except for the fact that it's always raining

Except for the fact that I'm the only one playing

Except for the fact that it's dark and gloomy

Except for the fact that in the game there is no feeling

Accepting the facts is how you play my not so very fun video game

<h1 style="text-align:center"><u>Sickbay Stay</u></h1>

Quiet it beeps

Silent I speak

Worried he sounds

Sympathy all over

Unsureness takes over

Quiet mumbles

Silent footsteps

Calling numbers

Winter under the cover

Unorganized lovers

Repetition takes over

<u>In the Crack</u>

In my dark room where I sat and stayed

There was a little light in the crack

The light in the crack kept on coming back

I pushed the light in the crack out

But the light in the crack came inside and sat

The little light in the crack became big

So the big light in the crack took up more space when it came in

The big light in the crack lit up the dark room in which I sat

I thank that big little light in the crack for always coming back

The Seashore Brought

On the sand where sadness stays

The seashore washes the sadness away

The seashore brought seashells of joy

All the sadness was no more

With the seashells, the shore brought a fish

And with the fish, I took care of it

With the fish, I went to the store

The little fish was lonely no more

Me and my fish shared the happiness

The happiness the seashore brought when it washed away the sadness

<u>What I Ordered</u>

Alone time in the trees

Swinging on the swings

Butter Pecan ice cream

Taking walks nightly

Dreaming of nice things

Eating healthy and rightly

Listening to my heart speak

Giving time to take it in and breathe

Buying myself pricey things

To let my heart finally breathe

I No Longer

I no longer look back on the sad times

I look back only on the good

I no longer cry past my bedtime

I lay back and think of you

I no longer look dull and sulk

My expression is filled with gladness

I no longer take in all the bad thoughts

My mind is only filled with what's good and true

I'm no longer the person after before

I am the person living in today

Afterall my fairytale ends with you and me dancing in the rain

<u>Ripped the Band-Aid</u>

The band-aid has been ripped off and suddenly I feel tough

The world can no longer push and sway and tear my emotions away

My foot is firm, and my chin is high

I will cry

Things won't be easy

But that is the experience of living

I've been to both sides

I've experienced it all

The hard, the tough, the weak, the rough

The unstable, the stable, the illusions, the feeling of walking on a cable

The ok and the not ok

The sinister schemes, the feeling of feeling below and beneath

I went through all the stages of grief

This is what it took for me to get back up on my feet

And yet sometimes I still feel without meaning

The difference is this destroys me no more

Because I am now newly freshly open to a new fresh world

Today, Yesterday, Tomorrow

Today I feel thankful for that I am still living

I am gleeful

I live in great delight

I pick the tomatoes in my garden

I go for strolls at night

Yesterday I went to the movies

I laughed at all the funny scenes

Yesterday I ate strawberries while looking at the scenery

Tomorrow I will hang with my friends

A joyful time of living

Tomorrow I might sleep in and enjoy the day's humble beginning

A Sight to Be

Sparkling in the sky a rainbow appears

Flying so high away from all cares

Chirping in the trees, buzzing are the bees

Blossoms of flowers a scent to smell for hours

Freshly picked herbs as the moon turns a bright white

A newly picked up book perfected from start to finish done right

Twirled from the sunrise

Twirled to the sundown

Reminiscing past times

Eyelids fall down

<u>Sunny</u>

Lightly brightly shimmering shining

Clearly aglow flashing fluorescently gliding

Vividly cloudless brilliantly rich

Incomparably lively, luminously shiny

Gleaming and glaring

Glittering and twinkling

Magnificently pleasing, alluring, and appealing

Gorgeous, stunning, splendid, and superb

Is your wonderfully lit beautiful smile

<u>Living Life</u>

I live my life in total bliss

I find my life harmonious

I know that I'm loved

I'm no longer alone

I carry on with life and happiness

Living life blissfully

I only need what I need

I picked up the pieces, piece by piece

I can now see what life has for me

I do not worry about today or tomorrow

I do not fill myself with sorrow

I find perfect happiness and great joy in store for me

I live my life in total bliss